ADRIENNE

A POETRY JOURNAL OF QUEER WOMEN
ISSUE O1

SIBLING RIVALRY PRESS
ALEXANDER, ARKANSAS
siblingrivalrypress.com

EDITOR
Valerie Wetlaufer

PUBLISHER
Bryan Borland

Cover art by Cindy Baker 2013. Used by permission.

Sibling Rivalry Press
13913 Magnolia Glen Drive
Alexander, AR 72002
info@siblingrivalrypress.com

Printed in the United States of America.

ISBN: 978-1-937420-65-9
ISSN: 2331-9194

Adrienne: Issue 01.
January 2014.

We encourage submissions to *Adrienne* by self-identified queer women poets of any age, regardless of background, education, or level of publication experience. For more information, visit us online at www.siblingrivalrypress.com.

POETRY BY

Judith Barrington

The Knot That Defies

READY OR NOT

When is anyone ready to face the moon,
to stride up the dark avenue and look
into inevitable light? Some have turned back
babbling of the whiteness they saw there,
the dazzle at the threshold she guards.
       I wasn't ready, they say.
       I had more to do, they say.

One in a million will be granted an extension.
The rest of us go on wondering when she will call.
She gleams behind a tree or above
the inverted V of the roof where rain putters—
each percussive drop a distraction from what must come.
When I've forgotten her altogether, out she hops
and locks onto my shoulder like an angry parrot.
       Her claws dig in.
       I'm not ready, I say.

LONG LOVE

Is it your legs I remember or that photograph of your legs?
Long and skinny they were, swooping from
tiny denim shorts to huge hiking boots
with bright red laces. It's a wonder those legs
could lift such boots, but they did, and with a grace
I cannot now attribute to love-struck eyes.

The thing is, when you grow old you fail to notice
your lover's legs very often. Love-struck gives way
to love-soaked, a softer state in which legs are taken
for granted—except if they appear without pajamas
in the kitchen or require a close look for a splinter
or a suspicious mole traced softly with your forefinger.

Feeling the brown spot, you are struck by fear—
love having grown by now into a world,
the mole a potential hazard that could split your globe
down the middle and leave it to float in space
like a white dwarf, as scientists call a dying star
that eventually leaves nothing but another black hole.

TYING THE KNOT

Mornings I threaded blue and yellow satin
over, under, slipped the end through the loop
and slid the knot up to my uniform collar.
I boarded the bus with a hoard of girls,
some with their ties loosely knotted,
some both feminine and neat; a few like me
more at home in this piece of butch
than anything we wore on Saturday night.

Now, when I venture out in a tie, I long
to board a bus and feel at home—
to strut down the street as I did at twelve
but the swagger is gone—lost except for the
practiced movements of hands at the mirror:
satin on satin, thread through the loop, then slide it up
to the throat: The knot that defines; the knot that defies—
the knot that knows how to brag but can also strangle.

WHAT KIND OF CREATURE

How can you miss someone who's always there
drumming his fingers on the dinner table,
turning his key in the lock at the same time each day?

In spite of their presence, in my generation the fathers
seemed to be missing, leaving us to wonder what kind of
creature a father might be—what feelings swirled

beneath the occasional rages, jittery impatience,
even the penchant for casting a line
into water where fish were said to lurk.

Mine was one of those unknowns—not that
I noticed his absence until later when I wondered about
those weekend days he spent alone in a rowboat

surrounded by frog song and wild azaleas,
throwing out his hand-tied fly and thinking.
Or did he perhaps go there not to think

but to cast out the contracts, the draftsman's arguments,
the need to smile at the elderly bookkeeper,
along with the lightweight line that played out

with the flick of his wrist and lay down feather-light
and straight, not so much as rippling the surface?
On those days, his head must have been filled

with nothing more than the smiling trout whose lips
sooner or later would swirl and grab, buckle the rod,
squirm in the net, and ease into shining death at his feet.

THE CHAPEL IN THE WOODS

I've never thought god lived in a church
but this chapel feels a little too godly—
a little like a home for someone or something.
Its A-frame roof and tall narrow window
imitate the triangles and trunks
of the pines outside sighing through their needles,
blending pine-scent with a faint incense
that swirls in the sunbeams.

I can hear birds but not the river,
wind and a distant plane, but not the murmur
of conversation; instead, there's the sound of
morning racing toward afternoon
as the river races down to the highway
past the postcard store.
But in here, nothing is going anywhere:
Is that the definition of godly?

Who inhabits this tree-made space?
Is it as holy as the cedar?
How can I silence my talking head
or speak to the emptiness
that even now is flooding into my spaces.
I simply don't know how to sit on this yellow pew
and not go anywhere at all.
It is to wood, not god, that I bow my head.

ELA BARTON

WORDS WERE OUR FIRST WEAPON

SCRABBLE

Every Sunday morning, Mikey wakes up early to watch
the games at the park. The field is a Scrabble board,
60-85 year old athletes, handling alphabet tiles like
Harlem Globetrotters.
This is not the chess games you see a few tables over.

Breathless pausing between knocks of knights and spawns
clicking and ticking of clocks between silent strategy
no, this is a cipher of the elderly, 11 point grandmas
turn 15 point grandmasters, these are versed veterans of
verbs. Weathered warrior wordsmiths, attaching scores to
skilled combinations of random letters.

His older brother, Andrew, took him to his first match
on his birthday. He gave him a dictionary, on the front
flap he wrote, "This is your first weapon;
choose your words carefully. Love Always, Andrew"
It was the perfect size for Mikey's back pocket.
Mikey swore on it like the truth, became the park

bench's law enforcement, catching phony words
and taking away turns like a Scrabble Sheriff.

He found his language one letter tile at a time,
deciphering combinations of letters like a code-cracker
discovering words tell you what they are if you
l-i-s-t-e-n- listen: 6 points
but to listen requires you to be
s-i-l-e-n-t silent: 6 points:
just rearrange the letters. Your ears with the same
letters can become the inlets to words if you
enlist them.

Four days after his birthday, Mikey found a letter by
Andrew to a friend.

It said words like John-14 points

love—7 points
awkward—18 points
gay—7 points
hope—9 points
do you like me back—33 points

Mikey never said a word.

2 days later, Andrew was found hung by his own belt in his
        bedroom.
Belt—6 points
suicide—10 points

After the ambulance removed him from his room
Mikey found another letter.

It wasn't in Andrew's writing.

It said words like Andrew—10 points

fuck—13 points

faggot—11 points
burn—6 points
hell—7 points
im going to tell everyone—31 points

Mikey never said a word.

At Andrew's grave site, Mikey played Scrabble.
He played sorry—8 points
brother—12 points

Mikey wrote his brother—12 points a letter to tell him he was
sorry he was silent.

Andrew—10 points
I'm sorry that I never said I love you.
I'm sorry his word score was higher.
If you listened to your heart it would have told
you he was a hater.
Just rearrange the letters.

Did you know that there are no perfect anagrams to "suicide"? All
I could make was "dies".

You will always be my perfect anagram—10 points
My Andrew—10 points

My wander—10 points

You warned—10 points me.

I'm listening
I'm silent

words will never hurt you now.

They've lied to us all along, Andrew.
Words were our first weapon
and they can kill.
I'm sorry I never said thank you.

Love Always,
Mikey

ARIZONA

In Arizona, law enforcement are allowed to ask
for proof of legal presence in the US
if there is any "reasonable suspicion."
What makes a human" reasonably suspicious" of not
belonging in one of the world's most ethnically
diverse nations? What gives anyone the right

to outline my features,
sample my skin color
and call it "illegal?"

They call me an invader
until I'm proven "free,"
telling me that
because I'm brown
I'll need proper ID.

Consider this my documentation:
First generation American citizen
but my family has always worked for you.
Our green cards are sown into your
plantations. Our papers are grown into

your pineapples,
your cotton,
your sugarcanes,
built into your railroads,
burned into your gold.

Identify my race. Tell me
where I come from before I even begin speaking,
then tell me to go back there.

Label me an Eskimo, brand me Mexican,
call me a Native American or something mixed
with "Oriental" like my uncle might have been a rug.

Consider this my documentation:
you've cut my ancestors' feet at the ankles
to keep them from leaving.
Identify me as invisible until

a crime is committed.
then identify me as the criminal.
Tell me this is simply for my safety,
then beat me,
then tell me I'm safe in Arizona,
when Senators are posing for pictures with Neo-Nazi leaders.

Tell me to just not break the law.

Have you ever been pulled over with a White passenger
and watched as a police officer questioned their safety?
Have you ever called the cops and they never came?
Have you ever called the cops and became a criminal?

Dear Senator Pearce,
When the Nazi Party crowned you
a "great statesman," did you feel heroic?
Did you see Superman in your reflection?
Is it the way his uniform and you wave red, white
and blue over the streets of Arizona?

Superman was from Krypton, Senator Pearce.
He was an alien.
No one ever asked him for his ID
because he was smart enough to be born White.
Welcome to Arizona, the Grand Canyon State welcomes
"Whites only." Marking people of color guilty until

proven . . .
free.

While refried bean smeared swastikas decorated Capitol Buildings
in Phoenix,
legal brown people are being marked reasonably suspicious in a
place
they always thought of as home.

We are not new to this.
We've been asked to deep throat your blaming fingers before.

The Exclusion Acts
Repatriation

Proposition 187
Repatriation
Japanese Interment
Repatriation

When we stop working for you
and start working for ourselves is when we no longer belong.
It's when we find ourselves standing on our feet
instead of falling to our knees.

Or is it all revenge, Senator Pearce?
Is it because an illegal immigrant shot your son?

Would I feel safer in Arizona if he was shot by a White man?

HARDWARE STORE

I'm at the hardware store.
And I know that I am not supposed to be here.
The men that are supposed to be here
have sawdust leaking from their pores,
paint stains on their pants
and buy beef jerky and drink mountain dew,
build decks in their backyards on Sundays.

They cannot bring themselves to describe me as a lesbian.
Because lesbians are characters in pornos, look good in
skirts, have Rapunzel hair and are pleading to be saved,
the dyke that just walked in does not really exist.

They cannot make their mouths cave in to call me woman.
Because why would a woman strap down their breasts like that?
Look awkward and full in shirts made for strong shoulders,
narrowing torsos. A woman, a real woman doesn't look like that.

Until they realize that it just might be true. That female
parts might still be hiding under these size 40 jeans. That I am
nothing but a pseudo she, a deformation of woman and man.

Do you know what it feels like to walk an aisle of eyes that
are disgusted, scared and pity you?
Do you know what it takes to be the woman that mothers pray their
children don't become?
A man is eyeing me in the lumber department. I can see
his macho swell in my direction, he does not know why
and neither do I but he has to let me know that he is a man . . .
He'll offer his help for no good reason, need 100 times the amount
of the product I want, scowl in my direction if I reach for it first.
He needs me to know that he is a man, and I am not.
I've seen this before. In the way straight men hug my wife,

wrapping testosterone forearms and biceps around her slender
curvy frame, pressing their investments against her breasts,
just in case she changes her mind about herself
and then they look at me . . .
bother up the nerve to give me their side, adequate space for
such a waste of woman, they hold me; roach in a tissue,
hoping to throw me away soon.

I know that I am a mother's cringe when daughters want to play softball,
the uneasy in your boyfriend when you use clippers on your hair, I am
the request for admission on ladies' night at the bar.
But I am not the blood sprayed across a smashed windshield,
so you have got to stop staring.
I am not sorry for who I am, so don't pray for my forgiveness.
I am not the bible, so do not go preaching your understanding
to anyone that will listen.
Do not call me sir or ma'am unless you'd like me to top you.
I am not to be deciphered.
We are so bloated with arrogance
we have forgotten that human is a taxonomic rank.
So selfish that we only believe in you or me.
I am at the hardware store
and I know that it has taken me years to get here. I can only
hope that the men that are supposed to be here
will get here soon.

EIGHT HOURS IN SIXTEEN STANZAS

clock in
bite tongue
swallow
work like you mean it
show yourself hard

cook pancakes and sausage
serve your future bosses
smile
wish them a great day
show more of your future bosses how to count change.

greet your younger, whiter boss
disagree with him about politics
watch your workload grow

julienne 75 bell peppers
wash your hands
trim the fat of 98 pounds of beef
wash your hands
smoke a cigarette

make 60 gallons of marinara
listen to your boss tell you all the things you could have if you were
younger
richer
straighter
whiter
wish that you could watch him reduce in a steam kettle

put meatloaf in the oven
put meatloaf in the oven

put meatloaf in the oven
listen to your boss tell you are doing it wrong
wonder how many ways there are to
put meatloaf in the oven

peel 72 potatoes
imagine your self-esteem a potato
imagine your boss as peeler
scrape
scrape
scrape
scrape
listen to your boss tell you are doing it wrong
scrape skin from your finger

bleed on 63 potatoes
throw them away
imagine yourself a potato
clean your wound
hurry up and clean your wound
looks like marinara

help the older women in the kitchen
memorize their hunch over chopping board
study their patience while they wait for retirement to add up
they will break even as well as their bones
while they wait with hunch that you begin to mimic

listen to your male co-workers and your boss talk about sports
notice they don't notice you
learn that they know more about last night's game than they do
about their jobs

check the time
curse yourself for checking the time
calculate how many work days are in a year

calculate how many work hours are in a week
calculate how much money it might take to survive this

watch your younger whiter boss raise his American voice
to co-workers who don't speak English
look at him look at you for approval
look at him look at you when you don't respond
watch your workload grow

clean up
clean up after your boss
take a brick to the grill
take pride in watching your efforts turn burn to silver
this is the only time you will shine

throw away extra food
feel your heart and stomach burn
remember the third world your relatives live in
remember you need eggs

remember you have no money to buy eggs
throw away 3 pounds of egg salad

take out the trash
lift 120 meals worth of scraps
into a dumpster
feel the bones
in your legs

in your back
in your feet
swing close to breaking

pick up your cutting board
wipe away with a wet towel today's work
sanitize your knife

watch the metal sharp glimmer as you wipe
notice the old in your hands

untie apron, place in pile
think about the employee who has to wash them
tidy up the area around it
release tongue from teeth

clock out

CHERYL BOYCE-TAYLOR

BROKE THE DOOR DOWN

BLUE HEART ZUIHITSU

once we moved in my lover would wake in the middle of the night
     saying
babe my back is itching
I would brush her back until she moaned and slept against the
     sloped howl of night

this afternoon after the mammogram my breast still stings from
     the shit of a machine named after a woman   Imagine that
no woman would create a contraption that could cause other
     women such pain
I walk through the farmer's market along Adam Clayton Powell
Plaza   the slight
pungent smell of fresh chard rosemary rhubarb tickle my nostrils
I move in closer to soothe my ache

South of London
I walk down Eddy Grant's Electric Avenue pass Brockwell Park
memories of Jay Day Cannabis Festival still hang lightly in the
     trees

1960's tie dye head wraps   cowrie shell earrings   floral bell bottom
jeans   in my beloved Brixton they recognize my Trinidadian lilt
right away   Scotch Bonnet peppers and jerk sauce on my tongue
my mouth tears into an East Indian mango red as sunset

she says she gets angry when I'm sick—she wants me
to put on my big girl panties (the ones I buy in bulk at Duane Reade) and take
care of my shit—
        last night she tore my skin   that's right tore my skin
    she should have worn a muzzle for this visit
in the water is a mirror   I see the bruise of her words take shape
claws then knives
bruise my small black—

"I was so alone the wind in my hair was enough to make me
weep." —David Lerner

two days of silence followed   two days of silence

      then my lover said
I don't really get angry
I get scared   can you forgive me
one
more
time   forgive—

I pass the lake   stand under the blueberry grove of trees
the hearts of berries stain the ground a deep blue

forgive me
she says

I tear my skin
I feel it open
expose the dumb gnarled pulp and slouch of the poet

hey my name is C and I go by she pronouns   later I will tell you

about mermaid
and the weeds in her tail for now there are adjectives up for sale

did I tell you I am a twin

now I cannot remember which self loved her so much
everyday less less
less less everyday less   every
day love her less
                    I remember the year I took my girl out for an exotic
                                father's day dinner
                    she was the daddy of our house then
the next year for father's day I made a Trinidadian Pelau with
crab lobster pigeon peas
I wanted to make it an annual tradition—
scallions mint leaves bits of mango chutney rice in coconut milk
then ginger-watermelon with raw honey on top for desert   I
served it on our living room floor clad only in my bare feet   an
orange bugle beaded Sari   and my blue fish eyed Bindi

—on the kitchen counter
   the glass table
the bathroom floor   holy god
praise tenderness
the sickle moon of her
bent against the faded light of the bedside lamp

still stops my heart.

TURKEY BASTING
FOR G.

she feeds me this broken city   from the spear of her fingertips
she no longer smiles a long constant cigarette sewn to her lips
how sharp you hold me now in the glassy river of your teeth   once
I scraped my womb   planted your two seeds   but our new shoots
drowned with longing   we smell the sea   your borrowed boots
kick up sand we eat
our dreams

what upsets you still lover   the child we never bore   trophy   flag
                              the womb dry as whalebone

CHICKEN SOUP

she would cut and season the chicken
chop the veggies days ahead

I'd dry the parsley leaves
roll cornmeal dumplings

slice garlic and ginger
cubes of butternut squash jalapeno pepper

she would gather all that was left over from the week
fridge bursting with scraps of carrots onions bits of chorizo

Sundays when we made chicken soup
in our kitchen of a thousand spices

Sunday times scattered about the kitchen counter
she pours a glass of our best vermouth

her tongue spicy in my mouth
a few sips later

she's a whirling dervish
giddy in her laughter

I am the olive in her dirty martini
her waiting car

her slick wet city street
teeth marks on my skin

ADRIENNE
ARRIVAL POEM FOR ADRIENNE RICH

Tonight Lucille and Audre
will hold hands

while waiting for Adrienne to come
just girlfriends arranging flowers

peonies hydrangeas baby's breath
Boston fern

summer quilts in the sun
pink lemonade swilled with fresh fruit

just girlfriends talking
about the glow of moon rock and the color of soil

it's possible we could go dancing
says Lucille, in her playful way

I propose some time for writing
says Audre, in her proper Carriacou twang

maybe there will be time after listening to new poems

tonight bed sheets will smell of sage
the kitchen of rice and oxtail stew

sister come, put your ear to my heart
hear the roar of that river called Adrienne.

WINE HOUSE

In second grade, we made paper boats
to sail when the river overflowed
after a rainstorm the sidewalk drain would fill
with angry brown water
taking with it marbles pebbles large milo tins
and our paper sailboats

in sixth grade
I wanted to fold my body into a paper boat
and sail into the arms of my beloved
a girl named Ammie with thick black glasses
and two well behaved braids
one over each ear with red bows plaited into each braid

after college I met the ballerina
her little toe was a tiny fraction of the first three
she used her toes as scissors to taunt
and shake her girls

she would pinch and tickle my nipples
with her toes all night
we howled obscenities to the stars
until we reached the wine house
and in one terrible thud broke the door down

LEO

I should have photographed the crack on the front door of my first home
how the afternoon light leaned in
I'd stand there taking in the warmth
watching the boys play soccer in the crisp dirt

for a long time I wished my son would have a baby
I even wished I'd have another baby with my new wife
it would be a boy we would call him Leo

I buried my son's first tooth near the wilting stalks
of the arsenic-blue salvia bush
so much ritual went into the penance of burying that first tooth

small pail of water
an old green plastic shovel
two sea shells one broken
the other perfect in shades of the palest carmine-pink
a piece of stripped peppermint candy
and a sliver of paper with the name Leo in slanted script
I called the tooth Leo

Leo was the caramel-brown boy
who shared his peppermints and orange with me
that first day in school
everyone called him sugar but I called him Leo

two weeks into the school year Leo disappeared from first grade
gossip had it that his father killed his mother and returned to
Venezuela with Leo
while others said his mother killed his father and ran away with Leo
whatever the story I always wanted to do a special ritual in his name

ZUIHITSU ON EATING POEMS
FOR JULIET

At fourteen
I learn the ways of poetry
how it enters your heart then hands full frame

the poem works it's way down my torso then up then out of my mouth
that glorious undeveloped mouth that only knows chap stick
   and girlish giggles
a mouth that knows simple words like hush no give

a mouth unknown to beauty
still innocent to the delicious pineapple of a woman's kiss
a mouth unknown to gossip and cruelty

at twenty
I fell out with my new husband of less than a year
my four-month-old son and I climbed into my mother's bed
she held me and read poems to us by candlelight

something in my heart shifts at the magic of her words my eyes
   filled with tears
mom reads Gwendolyn Brooks Sara Teasdale Edna St. Vincent Millay
she reads Derek Walcott Leopold Senghor and Langston Hughes
   a bud sprouts

the husband calls and calls
we do not answer
what holds me is this mystic painted doorway of words and the rich hum
of my mother's voice in the living room of these poems
a crop of words loop my heart there are azaleas and hibiscus
where the hurt used to be

Hibiscus-Rosa
lowers blood pressure

lowers cholesterol
prevents heart disease
the root soothes mucous membranes
Hibiscus flowers are also known as Jamaican Sorrel

as a child in Trinidad I drink sorrel
in Jamaica I drink sorrel and eat poems
decorate my windows with pink and red hibiscus
place hibiscus at the front door for abundance

I eat poems for breakfast
sprinkle poems on my honeydew melon
poems on my Inca Red Quinoa
I feed poems to my lover poems to my son he eats them like heirloom
tomatoes

later when he is gone I make murals of my poems
each poem painted with the Bulgarian-Rose of tree bark
the metallic pearl of patience
while the kettle hums I lure another string of words lithe like dragonflies
the wail of tribes ascending in the language of leaves.

TOOLS

A woman's body
has everything
to save her life

if you must
use your legs as oars
heel as hammer
teeth as machete

breast as flashlights
milk for building
monthly blood as healing salve

use your locks
to suture every wound
learn to cry
learn to speak

learn to speak
learn to breathe

learn to live within the smallest muscle of your heart

what I am saying is
let no one define your tools
your very necessary life.

ELIZABETH BRADFIELD

A FEW WAYS OF LOOKING

POSSIBLE REASONS

Because I should slow down.
Because I've been gone too much this year, traveling.
Because I'd taken health for granted.
Because I need a fire lit under me.
Or I've been too driven and have failed
to appreciate the domestic.
I've been fooling myself in those yearly forays back to Alaska to
        work. That's not knowing a place. Time to let go.
Despite the numbers I hadn't yet acknowledged my middle age.
Punishment for living across the country from my family.
Reminder to work better at building this home.

DEVIL FISH

I have never thought an airplane, even
one high and abstracted to a glint or
a holiday squadron executing
flips and turns, beautiful.
                              Once, staring
into the sea's afternoon lull, I saw two fins
rise up. Black surfaces toward each other, white
to horizon. Together, they disappeared, rose up,
and it took some time to remember the kite body
between them, the frowned mouth underside,
the whip tail's taper.
                        Home, walking the small loop
around the bog, alert to what rustles unseen,
I often hear the whine of fighter jets practicing.
Sometimes almost high enough to ignore. Sometimes
low and screaming a fierce joy at the stick.
                                              The rays
in the clear waters off La Paz look like a pilot's dream
of an airplane, fluid and alien. Sometimes they launch
from the water, flop and glint and then splash down.
And sometimes
                they swim in squadrons, as if
scales of some vast other form. I thrill a bit
to the gut when I see them. I resist
what syllogism wants me to concede.

AUGUST SONG

Hush the oak.

Hush the flood tide on the dry muck of the marsh

hush mind   hush heart

a yellowlegs hushes down on stiff wings

hush of water at its yellow knee-knobs

there's a hush to the sky: distance

and time will hush what hurt before.

What greater hush is there than a boat

aground then lifted by tide?

The planks the keel the gunwhale hushes to float

grass hush and locust hush pushed by wind

your frenzy does not quiet anything

your worry your ache fret grind

hush the days into sleep's relief

stillness at the core

that the wind stirs

as it passes through

leaving nothing but sound.

UNEXPECTED CONSEQUENCES
—1859

You invented the nephelometer to find smoke and
a respirator to help firemen save us from it.
You studied sound, designed a foghorn
to better warn us. You're John Tyndall

and have spent your days
building a spectrophotometer to count
the ethers of our atmosphere, then hunched hours
putting the numbers into conversation. *Ah,*

so it's like we're in a greenhouse—picture now
the potted palms and wild exotics brought back
from the world's jungles, root wads and stems
discarded as Victorians failed their care.

Swaddled in drapes and throws, your peers
thought Earth's cloud blanket welcome news,
a thing to muffle the damp and dank.

Every night, though, as Tyndall, you pour a little
chloral hydrate into a glass and drink it. You suffer
from insomnia, mind like the sun's unblinking.

Sweetheart fetch me . . . and she, Louisa, did. But
in attempting to help poured in too much. Your last
words as she fumbled drawers and shelves
for antidote: *My poor darling, you have killed your John.*

A FEW WAYS OF LOOKING

One hand-span wide
Safe on the table
The bear jaw is not my soul

*

In the morning, even the bear jaw
dreams of coffee, stained teeth
aching for the dark rush
that banishes dream

*

The bear stood up
from soapberries
and stared at me   Sun lit
its eyes caramel
I could not see its jaws
working

*

The psychologist
would call the bear jaw
desire: enamel cracked
teeth young enough
to be sharp

*

In my sister's house
there is no bear jaw
She is pregnant and has
lists of forbidden things
which she obeys
Her first sacrifice

*

My father would not want
a bear jaw in the house
Nowhere near it
That's the depth of his fear

*

Would a bear jaw
suit as talisman
to ward off boredom and ennui?

*

I think the bear jaw
laughs even as voles gnaw
its thinner flanges

*

Lower jaw   Left canine
chipped   Silt
rubbed into the crevices
Found

CONSIDERING THE PROPER MOMENT
TO DEFER TO AUTHORITY

The pilot announces delay, the left wing
tips into a circle, and the windows go blank.
I cinch my belt. The woman next to me
reaches for her bag, flips on her phone to check the time.

Suddenly, I think of the girls on trial in Salem,
faces gray and flat as low clouds, their accused selves
strapped into dowdy, pious, daily garb. The climate
that held them. And now the muddle of linkages:

I am the girls, captive; I am the Goody
deciding if what she sees is bad enough; I am the weather,
uncaring. I am pilot, pyre, judge, jet, nervous woman
whose English is just bad enough to make
the drone of announcements worthless.

I am the gap of understanding, the moment it widens,
the endless, shadowed fall of it, the figure mute on the edge,
maybe aware of future regret, maybe just curious to see if it's real.

ASSAIL

The wind comes up
suddenly, sometimes. As if
from nowhere. And all at once the bay

you've been enjoying—
tink of halyards on mast, tink
of glass rims, soft luff of sails, sigh

of hull on water—
completely forgetting the depths
and reach of, is mounting a surprise attack.

Ski-mask clouds.
Thunderbolt gun. No one I know
or want to know ever sees it coming.

CHING-IN CHEN

SHE WANTS YOU END-STOPPED

DESERT HUNTER

My water finish

                  high dunes   low desert

         Your microwave pores

                  flashcard response   to

                  precipitate   evaporated milk

                  lizard's tongue   coyote lie you

            I follow tracking

        the biologist   he the first

    trespass a measure

        tape the ghost

            a sneaker   No Humans

           Your palm empty

         droppings you

      crushed — your

    brittle fish

fry perfection   dry

             seeds behind baby

bumblebee

     wafer dirt rattlesnake

under ledge mustard

     grass flag wide

         beige field biologist hates Thunder

You cut
anyway hid
    in your knapsack

biologist's back ground-down   **Durian**
mountain invade grass   My field notes: this
                              coupling: grindice
       word "sea"   wide sigh through teeth
empty You distrust   listen, every tongue lacerate
  newcomers   tidy   granule   pungent nipple
                                 ripeskin
descriptions   long   pull   pucker lovestink
    familiar   own grown
internal language   water —   seedrough
                      resilient hair squeezejuice
                    suckbreath wake past belly
             to meet you

FRAGMENT QUEEN // SENTENCE LOVER

Raid night, she pulled up   figbar night market transactions
in front of my fruit stand, first and ready,   only inheritance family recipe
with chortling quarters. I took them into my   sisters knived in
hand, considering each one as if it were my   scatters after parents drowned
child. She stood close like a shiver, grinning   deep sea crossing   backroom immigration
up into me as I counted out the sweet things.
Then sirens and she wasn't in the mood.   deals   accumulated potato peelings   no
She usually liked to story and we needed a good parchments kept up in
long pull, afte Jose and Lee and Jimmy.   attic exists to gather her scrawled and close

Her brother through fire of van   all-night taqueria
shook his arms out for cuffs.   devours vowels   recites
She draped herself back into those   full sentences
                                       explains to a fragment queen
shoulders, waited out the night.   why she wants you
We slept on the tarmac, I missed her   end-stopped, like the bottom of a full
already.
In the morning, clear skies,   sea treasure
an empty soup bowl.   pot

THE SENTENCE DOLERS

Rumor says Monday in homeroom
that The Sentence Dolers will wait after
school to steal all our phrases.

I don't believe him. I go through
the whole day without preparing.

At the marble steps,
in frostpink bomber jacket,
short-shrift hair, one
shriveled arm and one iron-

pumped.

The rest flock to her snare.

I spare my sentence pare its lip
into the mouth of an envelope
pass it to her second-in-command

I cannot stop writing complete thoughts

Rumor or not

She faces me
her uneven arms   otherwise symmetrical face
hands stretched with
desire.

HOW OPEN HEART

		Surname	Given Name	Age	Race	Birthplace				Location
		reply we								
		small notes				*opening would be*				
		a flicker				*against the interests of*				

Throat

Note: uses borrowed language re-mixed from Srikanth Reddy, Keith + Mendi Obadike, Selina Tusitala Marsh, "10 Steps to Loving Others," 1900 US manuscript census.

Good life. Dress plainly. Moth, dusk, lightning (avoid), gongs (burnish). One   foot in front of the other,   to the filled pot. A friend tells me,
I could write poems maybe

DifficultThe **Other Side**

"strange stories" "hanging
from a death-dealing . . .
dressed in blue" "shuddered"
"trophy"

transactions. The third (count): enter, prosper, forward.

"the face, an ashen white"
"eventually spend one day
and one night" "congregate"
"around the collar and the body"
"besieged in Wisconsin"

Sun hides gathering season, everything picked dry

"a stuffed together
apparition" "simmering

by the time done arrives, dusted, sated with hours. Pickled

developments" "imposed

birds outside my door pennies

movement controls"
lined up a jar. Daughter
"stretching across four
days" "committed"
"threatening letter"
step. We turning a corner,

how you
"prisoner within"
at the ready, body full of
city. *"discipline"*

"what looked like a man"
"tendencies"

strain, maybe. Some days, a line isn't
enough to hold.

*Note: Italicized words from Victor Jew's "'Chinese Demons':
the Violent Articulation of Chinese Otherness and Interracial
Sexuality in The U.S. Midwest, 1885-1889"*

HUNTING ANCESTORS

brittle words
so concerned :: bottom rivers
                                    ironcast
                    pot.

She walked backwards —hard
to open :: A friend
                    tells me, I could

your fingers, but there ::

        write poems, I
think. Difficult

in the light, a graceful ::

        gathering season, everything picked dry. Hungry,
                                    my door

                                    step. We
                                    pickled birds
                                    outside
                                    turning a
                                    corner, how you

                        strain, maybe.
                        Some days, a line
bowl

                        enough

MEG DAY

GETTING CAUGHT STARING

PORTRAIT OF MY SELVES AT TEN, AS FATHER & SON

By noon, even the shock of pale skin that creeps
above the waistbands of their cut-offs
is strewn with the welts of mosquito bites,
their shirtless torsos browned by sun or dirt
or both. He has gathered smooth stones for skipping

& she has supervised, keeping one hand on her hip,
flipping a tangerine into the air with the other.
When the rocks continue to break the surface
instead of bounce against it, her shadow melds
to his, edifying. *Fit it to your palm*, she tells him,

making her motions his. *Cradle its edge
like you would the bent breath blown from a harmonica*,
they lean back, *or the curve of a breast*, their hips turning.
Cup it like you would a hand around a moth, & it escapes,
taking a few long strides, like Peter, before sinking.

WHEN THEY TOOK MY BREASTS, I DREAMT OF ICARUS

When they took my breasts, I dreamt of Icarus
& woke each hour to the blurry hands & heads
of Briareus in a white coat struggling to keep my arms
from flapping & the mercury in its glass.
They had lost me on the table, or so Icarus said,
& in the slow-motion scramble for paddles
or pulse, we flung our bodies, arms widespread,
& flew a flat line to the sun in brilliant exodus.
I, too, am the son of a craftsman, I told him later
at my bedside, *a master of time & the pieces that keep it.*
We spit, then, & shook, palms all wax & feather,
two brothers proved failures in such lineages of merit.
That night he slept behind me, our curved spines yawning
& when the sun rose they punctured both lungs to keep me from drowing.

When the pain was too much, they gave me Icarus
& he'd sit beside me while they emptied my drains,
or sing refrains of Fugees covers while doodling airplanes
flying close to the sun. He'd question my sutures,
Are you killing him softly with your song? & fall
to the floor in fits of laughter, my smile brighter
when we knew the cancer'd gone. *You'll be lighter
without all that weight*, he told me one night from the hall
& I lay alone in the dark watching the IV drip,
knowing he meant breasts & not the tumors that took them,
a flat-chested emblem of our future flight in tandem,
a handsome membership to—no, abandon ship.
I never wanted to be less woman. But I was
more monster than man, a leviathan in gauze.

When he fashioned my new breasts, Icarus did not use wax
or feathers, wristwatches or wings. He used caution & hesitation
& the cauterizing of things; he slapped warning labels on my decision,
instructed judgment to form a line at the door. *If you relapse
it'll be the last time*, he continued, miming the surgeon, scalpel in hand.
I've always said hubris was stored in the chest & they stitched in my pride,
one bag for each side. Later, when the drains were replaced & the sutures
retied, he asked if I ever thought about death: *Pearly gates? A big brass band?*
When I die, he said, *I hope I go in autumn; I hope I leave
with the heat of the sun still burned brown at my nape
& the thick gusts of equinox searing up under my cape;
I hope there is ocean enough for my scattering, & still sea left to grieve—*
O, how I'd come to crave the surprise of death instead of its prediction:
let me amazed by my departure, let it be some unafflicted eviction.

PSALM FOR JULY

Lord, call up the flies. Exhale them
in hot droves to hive in the skull
of a calf's carcass limb-sprawled
on the side of the road that meets

the road always trailing the Spiral
Jetty. Last spring, its hooves
cut snow angels in the stiff frost
icing the pasture—& scraped

at the glassed terrarium of dirt
July made bare with her drough—
until the chuff of cold cud rang
against its dogie teeth & the hard thud

of its head against the frozen mud
was swallowed by the famine wind.
How droll that July refuses the sweat
of labor—as if she were an idle sun

around which the seasons orbit—
& leaves the wiry beast to wither
without decay, to shrivel instead of rot,
its veal embalmed by ice & her neglect

even now. July, July: what ghosts
there do remain? Lord, rally the pests
& vermin; assemble their zealous mouths
in the cavities of her quiet ineptitude—

if this runt of a heifer can outlast
the hot hook of July, let my heart
be similarly preserved. Let this year
of bitter abandon leave me Ferdinand

in the face of her red cape façade.
Let the heat of those creatures'
hunger salvage all they can for reuse
& devour what remains, disappearing

that body into the earth & renovating
it like the bulb that breaks ground
despite the rime: there one minute—shooting
green—& reborn in blossom the next.

TAKER OF THE TEMPERATURE,
KEEPER OF THE HOPE CHEST

A SESTINA FOR SAMYAHSATTVA

Some have children in more foreseeable ways:
cesareans, episiotomies, long hours of labor
or paperwork, adoptions that often take years.
My girl, she came to me when the rope burns
on my brother's neck were still fresh from his hanging,
the noose tied up in the knots of her mother's

tourniquet, needles still cluttering the floor. Mothers,
I've been told, are not born but made—always
runners of the tight shift, leavers of the light on—hanging
one hat up only to put on another, their labor
of love still & always labor. What candle burns
at both ends & lasts the night? We did not have years

to find our rhythm; we did not have yesteryears
to lean on or call up, nor succor, neither of us mothers
to phone with a thermometer in one cheek & the burns
of death's whiplash on the other. Some lose children in conceivable
        ways:
bee stings, enlistment, the bloody shock of difficult labor
that comes months too early & leaves every head hanging

in the waiting room. My girl made her great escape from a car
        hanging
upside-down over a freeway divider, all twelve of her years
broken into as many pieces, a puzzle of bone no surgeon's labor
could solve. Sorrow, I have learned, is long-legged like our
        mothers,
& stalks me with a glacier's patience. It sits in wait. If there are
        ways
of burying a body—still breastless & birdlike & fresh with
        sunburns—

no mother ever taught me how. If there is grief so torrid it burns
the mother out of you, I have known it. Her coat is still hanging
in the hall closet as if she, too, returns home with us on the subway
after stacking stones to sit by the window & stare. Years
ago, I dreamt she had broke free of the soil, face—like her mother's—
pale as a bar of soap. She padded into the kitchen to belabor

the leaky sink: its quiet drip that refuses the plumber's labor
& remains, like a stray dog at the door. Sometimes the sound burns
like sun through a magnifying glass into the middle of my mother-
less dreams, tapping at the ache found pregnant & hanging
between the ticking second hand of the mantle clock. Years
of sometimes have made me cautious of bus stops & railways

& other laborious intersections of bodies & speed. Unchanging
now, like my own mother, I am afraid of sleep. Instead, I layaway
& awake in the burn of night, my womb a bed no one's slept in for years.

AFTER GETTING CAUGHT STARING, TWICE

Here we are again. I am holding half an acre of Michigan
    in my left hand, the map in soft focus behind us.
        You, you are Pacific headband & Ohio
        heartland,

touching Toledo to your chest like it wasn't a place we'd
    ever said aloud.
        In the attic, the bats are unfolding awake. Your
        look is fenceless:
            coke bottle glasses, eyes wandering behind
            the rims

like tropical fish. I do not notice the short frets of your
    spine in this dream,
        do not think to fingerprint your bedrock, do not
        feel the rumbling
            of honeypot ants gathering crumbs down
            the length

of my torso, waiting for the shiver of our first winter
    together
        to salt & pepper shakedown decades later, no. In
        this dream,
            our knees bristle against the carpet
            stubble

& I do not notice the humidity hugging your top lip.
    Your smile is broken, & the moons
    of my thumbnails slide
            between the folds of the Midwest.

HANKER IN RABBIT-QUICK HEAT

Want arrives ravenous & with talons, ferocious when ferocious
still means feral. Not circus-trained, not come-when-called,
not manageable-if-leashed. It hunts. Even in snow, it roots for
me. Winter is its sharp tooth, waiting for a body to size its bite;
winter is the tine-knitted mouth that shapes the hot hold of
breath between powerlessness & drive. It bent my will & broke
me, the way one breaks a wild horse to halter: tame under the
right conditions. It hounds my heart. It foxholes my hunger. To
be cornered by one's own howling: to finally feel the pleasure in
devastation: to be bucked, to fly, to land on hot, hard-packed dirt
that, like most things, feels too intact to leave: the red dust so
supple & the warmth of the sun so good.

PORTRAIT OF MYSELF AS I HAVE ONLY MET IN NIGHTMARES

I.

In the dark, because the body is always dark,
each cell lifts from another's back pocket or purse
a damaged inheritance that means nothing
without its stock, this human a store room
for pickpockets & bootleggers like us. What we are
is duplication: less virus, more hoarder,
the accumulation that matters & not the content of its glut.
We make variance imperceptible: like a buried tooth,
transgression is inborn; disaster smirks its potential
like black ice. Thrown against one another in the earth
of a figure built to replicate, we assemble & sow recklessly
uncertain of anything, save hunger & speed.

II.

The fever hit long before my knees met the floor,
the caps cracking with each shuffle toward
the door, the tacks coming up through the shag
in sharp swings of a baseball bat or boot, echoes
of other bones that have broken on other nights
tangled in the far-off echoes of her shower
humming, hymns tumbling out through the melee
of bullets & barking & faces beaten for resting
atop wrong bodies, bodies resting in their own blood
on sidewalks & bathroom floors, & all of it
soaking into the wallpaper we thought, at first,
must be textured but now, having dragged my slick cheek
against it in a slow-motion dune crawl across the carpet,
can confirm is flocked: stale & serpentine, pressed
like a flower, until all signs of life have been exhausted.

III.

In the waiting room, I read that solar winds
are blowing away the moon's topsoil & I think
I know what it's like to witness that first layer—
the most familiar—as it's pulled away
like sunburn, like snakeskin; I think I know
what it's like to watch a face go extinct.

AS MY SISTER GOES ON BED REST AT THIRTY-TWO WEEKS

IT'S AS IF THEY PUT [LAIKA] IN A METAL WOMB
& COOKED HER ALIVE WHILE SHE BEGGED
TO FEEL THE EARTH AGAIN.

There were others before her:
sent into sub-orbital flight,
they stayed on course
long enough to succumb
to stress or heat, every screen
eventually quiet with speculation
& disbelief.
    When they conceived
of the idea, they weren't expecting
she'd survive; but if Sputnik's sequel
required only four weeks to build
then certainly, having borne so much,
she can resist gravity that long.

LAURA HERSHEY

THE VIOLENCE OF STAIRS

1 KING BED, NON-SMOKING, CONFERENCE RATE, ACCESS

We knew we had between us three
skilled hands and tongues and hearts.
Two of us could hear; each could see

the words we lipped like ghee
with the code-cracking arts
we knew we had between us three.

You here, you there, between you me.
Honor our pauses and restarts.
Two of us could hear; each could see

and teach without etymology
words for waken, strum; the quaking parts
we opened up between us three.

We sucked and spilled our Snapple tea,
theorized what cripqueer imparts
of we who talk, fuck, hear and see

against norms, and claim authority.
In sticky sheets we rose like tarts
to know again between us three
a burst of want we cried to hear and see.

TELLING

What you risk telling your story:

You will bore them.
Your voice will break, your ink
spill and stain your coat.
No one will understand, their eyes
become fences.
You will park yourself forever
on the outside, your differentness once
and for all revealed, dangerous.
The names you give to yourself
will become epithets.

Your happiness will be called
bravery, denial.
Your sadness will justify their pity.
Your fear will magnify their fears.
Everything you say will prove something about
their god, or their economic system.
Your feelings, that change day
to day, kaleidoscopic,
will freeze in place,
brand you forever,
justify anything they decide to do
with you.

Those with power can afford
to tell their story
or not.
Those without power
risk everything to tell their story
and must.

Someone, somewhere
will hear your story and decide to fight,
to live and refuse compromise.
Someone else will tell
her own story,
risking everything.

THIS POEM WAS ORIGINALLY PUBLISHED IN THE CHAPBOOK
SPARK BEFORE DARK (FINISHING LINE PRESS 2011)

TRANSLATING THE CRIP

Can I translate myself to you?
Do I need to?
Do I want to?

When I say *crip* I mean flesh-proof power, flash mob sticks and wheels in busy intersections, model mock.

When I say *disability* I mean all the brilliant ways we get through the planned fractures of the world.

When I say *living in America today* I mean thriving and unwelcome, the irony of the only possible time and place.

When I say *cure* I mean erase. I mean eradicate the miracle of error.

When I say *safe* I mean no pill, no certified agency, no danger to myself court order, no supervisory setting, no nurse, can protect or defend or save me, if you deny me power.

When I say *public transportation* I mean we all pay, we all ride, we all wait. As long as necessary.

When I say *basic right*s I mean difficult curries, a fancy-knotted scarf, a vegetable garden. I mean picking up a friend at the airport. I mean two blocks or a continent with switches or sensors or lightweight titanium, well-maintained and fully-funded. I mean shut up about charity, the GNP, pulling my own weight, and measuring my carbon footprint. I mean only embrace guaranteed can deliver real equality.

When I say *high-quality personal assistance services* I mean her sure hands earning honorably, and me eating and shitting without anyone's permission.

When I say *nondisabled* I mean all your precious tricks.

When I say *nondisabled privilege* I mean members-only thought processes, and the violence of stairs.

By *dancing* I mean of course dancing. We dance without coordination or hearing, because music wells through walls. You're invited, but don't do us any favors.

When I say *sexy* I mean our beautiful crip bodies, broken or bent, and whole. I mean drooling from habit and lust. I mean slow, slow.

When I say *family* I mean all the ways we need each other, beyond your hardening itch and paternal property rights, our encumbering love and ripping losses. I mean everything ripples.

When I say *normal* I don't really mean anything.

When I say *sunset,* rich cheese, promise, breeze, or iambic pentameter, I mean exactly the same things you mean.

Or, when I say *sunset* I mean swirling orange nightmare. When I say *rich cheese* I mean the best food I can still eat, or else I mean poverty and cholesterol. When I say *promise* I mean my survival depends on crossed digits. When I say *breeze* I mean finally requited desire. When I say *iambic pentameter,* I mean my heart's own nameless rhythm.

When I say *tell the truth* I mean complicate. Cry when it's no longer funny.

When I say *crip solidarity* I mean the grad school exam and the invisible man. I mean signed executive meetings, fighting for every SSI cent.

When I say *challenges to crip solidarity* I mean the colors missing from grant applications, the songs absent from laws. I mean that for all my complaints and victories, I am still sometimes more white than crip.

When I say anything I know the risk: You will accuse me of courage.
I know your language all too well, steeped in its syntax of overcoming
adversity and limited resources. When I say *courage* I mean you sitting
next to me, talking, both of us refusing to compare or hate ourselves.

When I say *ally* I mean I'll get back to you. And you better be there.

THIS POEM WAS ORIGINALLY PUBLISHED IN MAKE/SHIFT: FEMINISM IN TRANSFORMATION, ISSUE 9: SPRING/SUMMER 2011.

JP
HOWARD

LET ME ENTER THE ROOM
ON MY TERMS

GHAZAL FOR HER VOICE

Life is a circle, weaved
around fragments of her voice.

I keep entering an empty room;
drawn to memory of her voice.

Where would she be today,
if I hadn't cut the cord to my voice?

Tomorrow when she wakes,
I wonder to whose voice?

One day I will break this cycle and
silence these shattered voices.

Tonight someone whispered, Juliet,
wrapped in echoes of her voice.

149TH STREET, SUGAR HILL, HARLEM

When I was seven, I had my first crush on my friend Yvette,
who adults all said looked like a young Lena Horne,
all I know is she was pretty and liked to play dress up with my
      Barbie dolls.
Mama was tough and smart.
When Peanut's cousin, who everybody said got high all the time,
robbed Mama and me in our elevator,
Mama yelled "Muthafucka just take the money!"
He didn't even realize
Mama made sure to take her keys out her little purse,
before turning it over.
I didn't ride elevators again for ten more years.
Our scraggly gray poodle Squeak-Squeak didn't even bark.
Mama said he was a little good-for-nothing pet, but I still loved him.
When me and Tiffany dropped water balloons
from my third floor apartment on our crotchety neighbor Mrs. Long,
Ms. Janet told on us and we both got our butts beat that summer.
It was worth watching old Mrs. Long's wig fall off her shiny bald head.
When folks started calling our neighborhood Hamilton Heights
we all said that sound too fancy. Anyhow, when summer heat gets
      too hot
for our tiny apartments, old men still pull out their folding chairs
      and sit on the stoop.
We still Sugar Hill.

FOUND POEM: FOR TRAYVON

The man in the video
had no intention
of target practice.
He confirmed:
a company offered for sale a target,
a faceless silhouette
wearing a hoodie,
his hands in his pockets,
one of which was holding two objects.
These objects were non-threatening.
The target was acting suspiciously.
His faceless silhouette was a novelty.
The man shot the silhouette in self-defense.
His intentions have been misunderstood.
He didn't think it was appropriate
for "a no-shoot situation."
Authorities confirm the target was unarmed.
He was a silhouette,
wearing a hoodie,
his hands in his pockets,
holding two non-threatening objects.
He bore a likeness to Trayvon.

Found Poem: The words in this poem are taken from an ABC News article entitled: "Trayvon Martin Shooting Targets Were 'No-Shoot' Tools, Fired Cop Says"

M   R
   A   K   IT   UP

if this poem could talk she would S C R E A M:

muthafuka don't write me in no fuckin form
don't write me in haiku, cinqku, sonnet or that tercet
shyt
please whateva you do **DON'T TRY &**
SOUNDMEOUT!
Let me ramble onandonandon……………..get alla
this anger out let me spread my stuff all over the page
do not hem me in between some fancy ass words

let me enter the room on my terms

if you must push me up on
some syllables don't let those
suckas rhyme leave that for
all those fancy forms that

                    drop in journals. i've got my
own style

        RESPECT!!!
if this poem could talk she would
    wrap herself around your throat
      burn as you swallow her whole
        tag your vocal chords with blood red spray
paint:

SHE WAS HERE.

I AM

i am dyke bulldagger lesbo femme butch lipstick lesbianboi lez gay
queer aggressive androgynous soft butch femagress lezzie bulldyke
diesel dyke baby dyke stealth dyke drag dyke bear dyke trans dyke
spiritual stud soft boi bean flicker carpet muncher muff diver
pussy puncher todger dodger lesbian homo pungent scent hard
nippled loud moan soft nibble tongue nape of neck whispered
earlobe pulled loc melted dark/milk/white chocolate wet lipped
cocoa butter round rubbed tattooed back sweet ass ready to be
rode spanked licked fucked pushed poet woman.

EIGHT LOVE POEMS

Year 1
Our first night in my studio in fort greene
you whisper in my ear: *I am willing to wait for you.*
i don't ask for how long.
this won't last more than six months.
it never does. it's ok i say.
tired of always running into myself.
will you catch me next time?
i could stop wishing us into existence.
will i forget how to write if i'm happy?
you are the first to challenge me.
no one has ever made me make a choice before.

Year 2
You discover i hate mornings.
cannot wake up in time,
when we stay in your jersey apartment.
this will not work. not like this. i always get my way.
the curse of the only child. we compromise.
Juan tells us about his building. five minutes from our jobs.
we love it. that first night
in our first apartment together
we stand barefoot in our bedroom
on the powder blue carpet.
lights from the brooklyn bridge welcome us.
we are home but i'm still worried.
will you leave next year?

Year 3
You are a jersey girl at heart. but this city is growing on you.
or is it me that has grown on you?
we walk on the rocky beach in provincetown in june.
we decide we will retire here,

open our own bed and breakfast one day.
we hate new york winters. we crave sand and warm water:
aruba in february.
the waiter in the hotel restaurant asks if we are sisters.
we say no and laugh when he leaves the table.
back in the room we shower together
sisters don't touch each other like this
you whisper in my ear as i fall into you.
maybe you will catch me next year.

Year 4
I panic when i realize all our monies are commingled.
when did this happen?
i add this to my list of issues to work out in therapy.
you watch me sort through the baggage of my past without judgment.
each day i find a new part of myself and share her with you.
this is the longest relationship i've had.
this year we talk about wanting children.
i want to be the mother i wanted.
in our house, there will be no scent of stale beer
and cigarettes behind closed doors
while a child waits, on the other side, for daylight.
you have learned from her mistakes, you reassure me.
we stay up all night thinking of names for our unborn child.

Year 5
We order four vials of donor sperm #417.
we have no idea what we're doing,
even after months of pouring over long lists of anonymous donors.
i can't bear to look at the result after the first insemination.
you scream loud. kiss me a thousand times when the plus sign appears.
we cannot stop crying.
this is a year of change.
you read langston poems to my belly.
i write odes to you and baby and dream of lavender picket fences.
at the city clerk we register. our baby kicks for the first time. approval of

this union.
each year on our anniversary you will tease me
about this shotgun wedding.

summer's coming
summer can't come fast enough.
sweet warm sticky translucent waters
fall without warning.
you cut the cord.
we take turns holding Jordan.
he feels familiar to us.
beautiful brown skinned boy.
today is the beginning.
no paths to follow.
an open door and a man child that we have always loved.
together we will catch him if he falls.

Year 6
The ticket agent at the airport doesn't believe us
he cannot have two mothers. two women in the world with a man child
i can still see the look of shock when we show him Jordan's birth
         certificate.
two women. two parents. it was funny that first time.
but this will not be the last time we have to prove our existence to the
         world.
death comes close. your mother struggles with cancer.
i hold you. we help her fight for life.
we watch. your mother grasps air holds on.
we can exhale. this year death passes us by.
for the first time, i am learning the dimensions of family.

Year 7
We have lunch together on the brooklyn bridge.
autumn frames our new york skyline.
tomorrow we will meet again, begin this new ritual.
tomorrow doesn't come. only death.
i sit stranded on an uptown r train
as the world falls apart and comes together.
i exit to strangers friends strangers.
the towers have fallen. the towers have fallen.
strange soft women hug me on the street.
they wipe away my tears i wipe away their tears.
i cannot reach you on the phone.
i will you safe in your corner of this big city.
i walk silently over the manhattan bridge
with friends and strangers and friends.
bring colleagues to our apartment for water and rest.
you and Jordan walk through the door.
the world begins to come together again.

JOY LADIN

NERVOUS IN THEIR BEAUTY

CAFE IN CONCORD

Young women nervous in their beauty, overflowing
plates, fries and burgers, foaming ice-cream sodas, beaded water glasses.
In the next booth a handsome woman harangues
a close-cropped, sand-colored man.
Is it love that makes her so afraid,
is her whole life piled on the arm of his life
like the waitress' wobbling stacks of cutlery and plate,
am I looking down on her fear from above,
or, searching your face for love, am I exactly the same?
No food on the menu I can bear to eat. Meat
sizzles on the grill, screams out orders, waits.

INTIMACY

Poor baby.
Everything you are is wrong.
You're married, you have a home, a place

where everybody knows your name.
OK. But notice
how you move, juggling too much body

against not enough soul, adapting yourself to drowning
inner cravings
for beige, champagne and pink.

There are many ways
to reduce heart-related problems. This
isn't one of them. You've married yourself

to disconnection, a pile of laundry, a razor, a million reasons
to hold, repeat, suffer.
You turn out the lights and try to remember

how much you wanted to give her,
circling the old anxiety-created horizons,
wishing you weren't losing her love,

that love would launch you, side by side,
into the sky of a future
where you could end on a high note, together.

SOMEWHAT AFTER PUBERTY
FOR BARBARA DANA

Novice knitter, knit with us.
The divorce is finally over, paving the road
from crying more than usual

to the elegant, sensual, female side
of emotional intelligence.
Your odyssey of transformation

deserves sashes and broaches, extra needles,
florals and coral strands.
How many years has it been?

Wiggle the steering wheel,
crawl under the car
and take control of your body.

Forgiveness is all around you,
eliminating the unsightliness of adolescing
somewhat after puberty,

ensuring a smooth transition
as your hard-earned water drains
from soil into blossom.

The divorce is finally over, soul and body
have begun to knit, to kiss.
Novice knitter, bride-to-be—

Step into the goddess.

JOY LADIN

DUET

IN THE WOMEN'S ROOM

Chime of bladders emptying side by side,
pinked by tile, amplified,
dampened by wall, porcelain and thigh.

We can't see each other's faces
but we hear each other's sighs,
the music neither of us means to make,

the music of emptiness and fullness
randomly synchronized.

NATURE

FOR CHAIA HELLER

Three cheers for nature. Two and a half. One
for growing, one for dying, half for the tangle

of stem and seed, contingent and inevitable,
that naturally splays between

myths of perfection, balance, monstrosity,
tragic falls, reddened jaws, self-devouring chains of being.

It's our nature to think this way, unnaturally ascribing meaning
to what nature doesn't mean,

rooting for nature the way denizens of rusting factory towns
root for the home team, waving its flag, sporting its colors,

fondly shouting "we"
to undefeated golden seasons and decades of futility

and game-saving plays by kids
later seen bagging groceries

who stand for all we wish nature could
and know she cannot be.

ANOTHER FORM OF LOVE

We knew this would happen, that I would forget
how to talk to you, that you would forget
to want me to,

that our summers would split in two
as each of us remembered the pleasure
of walking around naked in upstairs apartments

where no one else is sweating, of feeling unknowable
        and unknown,
of time revolving around us like the private sky
of a world for one

sumptuously appointed with beaches and stones, grocery stores
and bicycle pumps
and constellations of nameless others
who rise and set, dim or shine, with the charming irrelevance
        of stars,

and, blinking across the void,
tell us all we care to know
of where and who we are.

LETTER TO A FRIEND

Yes, I'm trying to help you
by hinting that you are drowning
in an outgrown idea of freedom
as I once drowned in the remains, thick as draperies,

of an idea of marriage. Foxed by depression, age
and a hundred crashing discrepancies—
loss of species, loss of name—
I might not be much help, but I am trying.

At times hilarious, at times erotic,
you, I hint—I don't know how else to say this—
are still so guarded as to be nearly latent, your freedom beautiful
but minuscule, a pebble stamped with a destiny

you don't know how to read. Your youthfulness, at least,
is in fine condition: your love of books, your affectionate wit,
the bevelled innocence of your life, shining with love
and fear of love, that is the fear of death.

PLAIN OLD FOREVER

Death, shmeath—
Been there, done that, conceived and aborted
innumerable futures
in a single breath.

Eternity curves and recedes
like a cheek you blush,
highlighting the contour of the bone
where being meets nothingness.

Even forever has a flavor, invisible and sweet, like a small ripe fruit.
Even nothingness creates a sensation,
like a pushup bra maximizing cleavage
between spirit and matter.

You were fine while you lasted, you're fine
fading from lilac to black,
you'll be fine when you stop shopping and sweating
and slip into something more comfortable,

Earth that fits like a moccasin,
plain old forever
sliding over your head
like a cotton dress.

PRACTICE EROTICIZING

WHAT DOESN'T NEED TO BE

What Comes Pouring Out

There is a party. A building made of concrete that spirals. The top two or three curves constitute a roof. The party qualifies as a roof party.

I am at this party, mostly trying to avoid a woman I once loved and once nearly was. I am also trying to avoid all others that know this. Meanwhile, I act as a gender mentor to a few young people. At this party, folks wear IDs around their necks with words and images describing their selves and preferences. I am helping these young folks build false documents. People call them falsies, though no one seems to have an original. People wonder why I am not the government agency in charge of hanging identity documents. People wonder if I am.

WHAT DOESN'T NEED TO BE

What Grips Like Not Wood

There is a storm. We should evacuate the huge spiraling concrete tower, but the curves cost a lot of money for the host to rent. Guilt keeps us all there, gluing us to one another. The storm is also shaped like a spiral, the inverse of the tower. When the two spirals meet, they lock into each other like the dovetail joins on the rocking horse in the basement. The storm has a lot to hold on to. When the storm starts moving back upwards, it stretches the building along with it. The concrete spiral changes shape, pulling up and away and toward. The partygoers go, too, sucked up into. When the storm lets go, the building snaps back, the concrete spirals collapse onto themselves. The survivors begin to unfold them, to look for more. We find pieces of clothing, empty, without their people. The people in the towering buildings surrounding this one assume there are no survivors, don't come looking. It starts to get a little Lord of the Flies in there, over the one surviving toilet paper roll and the somehow functioning floorplan a few levels down from the concrete folded like fabric. I start to inventory the survivors. I am looking for the woman I loved once, who must have been at the party, and maybe she is here. She is not. My mentees are present, but their falsies have been sucked away.

We know how these storms carry. We know that there is a place up there like Oz or Kansas in the sky, and if we want to find more survivors, we must go there, to in the sky.

WHAT DOESN'T NEED TO BE

To Launch a Rescue Operation

When we finally plan for it, we pull the rubberized once-concrete folds down into the surviving building, strap ourselves between the folds, and use the once-upper floors (pulled down into the once-lower floors) as a gigantic, impractical slingshot. This works, of course. We land in the beautiful other. We are welcomed. Up there in the sky, they've been product-testing progressive children's toys. The party is there. They are nude. We are nude; our slingshot went back to the down there with our clothing. We are prepared to act as inventory checkers, to place our number 32 stickers into garments and onto metal puzzles. When I spot her, she smiles that smile like we were each other's. The kind of recognition you look away from. The keepers of the up there say if we inventory sticker-placers want to take the product testers back down, there is only one way: we will all be ejected into the out there, all at once. We will need to use our collective body as a wide net, catching and then joining hands. When we have collected enough bodies from the ether of the out there, our collective body will gravitate to the back down. This is all or nothing. At first, our net will be not wide enough, but then, too quickly, too heavy to control.

WHAT DOESN'T NEED TO BE

To Be a Body Within a Body

I catch her easily on the way into the out there. Colliding with her body feels. We have formed a collective body already. We extend to catch a few friends, a few mentees. We see, a few feet off, the woman my woman loves. The friends on that end are tired. I am filled with the specific dread that if we don't catch her, this woman and I will be joined again. The weight of this adds to our collective body. I shove my left arm, thinking about extracting my body from the collective. I've shoved the friends on the left to the left. We float down, to the left. The friends extend their arms in a chain. The woman joins our collective body, and we go down like a breath.

WHAT DOESN'T NEED TO BE

What Recovery, In What Was Not Wanted, Owns

We are back in this place. It seems it's ours now. A roof garden has grown from the party spoils. My woman who is not mine handcrafts overly organized stalls from the rubber not-roof, a marketplace for the neighbors down below. We live in tents made from the textiles of the stall sides, of the clothing not claimed. The tower neighbors nearby still have no interest. The not-spiral tower is for no one else now. We've earned the place, I guess, or the glue of it. I feel out of. I feel within. I wonder if she.

DISCOVERY NARRATIVE

AN ACT IN FIVE PLAYS

origin

My shirt removed. A naked sculpture. I am encased in surgical mesh, my armature showing, stripped down to this. I am asking you to puzzle over me. The parts of me that are attractively masculine when clothed, attractively feminine when nude, are grotesque in this moment. I am packed into myself. The most naked I can be. I want you to help me out of my binder. To know what this is.

practice eroticizing

The pilot is unwilling to understand pain. He asked me to dress up like a boy for him. When he stripped me, he grabbed my chest through the mesh and grunted. He peeled my binder over my head, then the compression layer worn beneath. And then he grabbed them, gripping. I shoved him off; he landed on the bed casually, casually gazing. I squeezed my breasts, coaxing circulation or pleasure. He insisted he could be gentle; he began again. I came in one particular moment of pain, clamped my teeth down on his shoulder; he moved my face away, chiding, "No pain." Bruises like his fingers for a week.

when I was not the other

I was other in a lesbian bar, but dancing. And then against the wall. Mouth on mouth. My fist gripping abdomen, finding the familiar friction of shirt against binder there. I gripped harder then. Kissed harder. Placed fist on my abdomen, my friction.

avoidance

I do not always bind when we are together. My body does not always bother me when we are together. I would like you to read my body with your fingertips, to glean information from my sounds. I imagine your hands upon me, cool and soft on my scars, my parts. Trace me, my rough-hewn assemblage resisting female form. Trace me. I will not be afraid.

encounter

I imagine my body under your body. You slip your hand shyly under my shirt like a teenager. Instead of cool skin, you find warm mesh; it slips firmly against. Friction under your naked hand. No spectacle.

TRAVELING
AN ACT

Scene
The streets are cobbled, and the boys wear newsie caps. I want to acquire one—a boy, or a newsie cap. The long sticks are curly, and they lie in a pile on the stones. Maybe they are for sale. Many of them are broken. The boys select sticks according to height.

I met two potential lovers on a micro-blogging platform, but they each live in separate dimensions which you can only travel between on flying bicycles pedaled with long sticks. They each look like the bully from that TV show or like my annoying neighbor who I am lonely enough to talk to or maybe even fuck. I get them confused with one another, bicycling between burger joints in different dimensions. In one dimension, there is danger. A shortage of sticks. Many newsboys traveling. In their haste, the boys start getting their bodies confused with the other boys' bodies. They find themselves suddenly pedaling another boy's bicycle with another boy's sticks held in another boy's hands. Nobody knows whose body belongs to whom. There is no longer any hope in me finding either of my potential lovers. They could be in anybody's body. No one is in my body. I select two sticks and ride home short and sexless.

TRAVELING

AN ACT

Scene
The locker room walls are lined with metal baskets filled with white shoes. The baskets are the kind yuppies special order from vintage-look wholesalers to decorate their homes with. The shoes are the kind no one is nostalgic for.

There is a woman there who wants me to try on all of the shoes. I insist this is ridiculous. She says the shoes are for the gymnastics team, and since I am the gymnastics team, I must try on all of the gymnastics shoes. I insist that I am not the gymnastics team, that the gymnastics team left in a bus full of girls. She looks at me, puzzling whether I am a bus full of girls. I am undressed for the shower. I consider covering myself in shoes. We each look around at each of the shoes. After a time, she walks through the doorway. She turns left.

TRAVELING

AN ACT

Scene
There is something like a spa there. The doorway is too wide and cannot be closed. The room is built for luxurious aesthetics and oblivious bodies. There are six tubs, maybe. Maybe a water fixture facade on the wall. Sinks. A closet with shelves. No doors.

The bathtubs are collapsible, which makes them difficult for bathing. The facility is singular, with specific times set in which men or women can use it. I sneak in between time slots. When I am in the collapsible spa tub, struggling in the plastic liner, naked on the floor, a beefcake stands in the wide doorway on his way to the racquetball court, and there is no hope for modesty. He stares at my chest. When I slide down in the tub to intersect my gaze and his, his gaze does not break. I am accustomed to this kind of gaze. I am still thrashing in the impossible tub. He walks off with his strange body in tow, considering my strange body. The closet fills with what is imagined and spills over. The spaces between the tubs are filled. The remaining plastics begin collapsing.

TRAVELING
AN ACT

Scene
The room is full of double beds. The beds are covered in those awful hotel quilted tapestry spreads. There is a bed fitted to a window frame. The frame is obsessively, delightfully, exact. The curtains are also quilted tapestry. The patterns melt into one another in the exaggerated pleats.

I am with an old friend and an older friend and a lot of people we know. I think, maybe I'll share the window bed with my old friend, but then I am in a top bunk with my older friend and I don't know where we are. We are topless and touching and she is a fantastic lover. She tells me what to do to her nipples, what to do with her breasts. I find this patronizing and arousing. I have the terrible pleasure of pinching one nipple away from her body, placing it on the wooden bed frame's edge, and rolling the heel of my hand across it, producing a violent twist. She shows me how to get the same effect in my hands, palm against palm.

The curtain slides down across our skin. When she comes, I stifle my screams.

LESLÉA NEWMAN

I CARRY MY MOTHER

SAFE PASSAGE

My mother is preparing
to depart and will soon set sail
without me. Standing at sea
I keep a close watch

as the gang plank is lowered
the whistle is blasted
the "All Aboard" is called
and my father steers

my mother by the elbow
his spindly legs unsteady
his scrawny arm
slung across her shoulder

which is anchored by the sea
green oxygen tank
that hangs there heavy
as a bag of wet sand.

On deck now, my mother leans
against the rail as she leaves
us in her wake
growing smaller and smaller

waving goodbye
one last time
her fingers fluttering
in the wind like a sail

my father beside me, waving back
his hand opening and closing
like a beacon
all is well all is well

and as we slowly start
to drift apart
and she journeys
toward a new horizon

I stand ashore, one hand
holding onto my hat
the other waving
for all I am worth

and though I am buoyed
by her love
which floats between us
like a lifeline

when she disappears
I taste salt
I come unmoored
the waves knock me down

THIRTEEN WAYS OF LOOKING AT MY MOTHER

I
Among seven silent rooms
in the middle of the night
the only moving thing
is a swirl of smoke
rising from the lit tip
of my mother's cigarette

II
My mother was of three minds
like the three sorry children
she would someday come to bear

III
My mother whirled through the kitchen
slamming drawers, banging dishes
clanging pots and pans
She was a noisy part of the pantomime

IV
My mother and her mother
are one
My mother and her mother and her daughter
are one

V
I do not know which I dread more
arriving at my mother's house
or leaving it
The pain of being with her
or the pain of being without her

VI
Knitting needles click and clack
as something wooly grows
My mother stares at her creation
Her mood is indecipherable

VII
Oh skinny blonde airbrushed models
staring up at my mother as she flips
through glossy magazines,
Why must you torture her so?

VIII
I know how to make matzo balls
big as fists
and how to live on nothing
but cottage cheese, cigarettes, and air
but I know, too
that my mother is involved
in everything I know

IX
When my mother moved
from Brooklyn to Long Island
she marked the edge
of one of many circles

X
At the sight of my mother
staring back at me
at three in the morning
from the unforgiving bathroom mirror
I cry out sharply

XI
I rode home on the train
and fear pierced me
in that I mistook
the phlemgy hacking cough
coming from three rows back
for the sound of my mother

XII
The ventilator is on
My mother must be breathing

XIII
It was twilight all day
and all night long
she was breathing
and she was trying to breath
my mother lay in the ICU
her hand in mine
holding on for dear life

HOW TO BURY YOUR MOTHER

Slip out of the dark limo
into the bright light of day
the way you once slipped
out of your mother:
blinking, surprised, teary-eyed.
Turn to your father
and let him take the crook of your arm
like the crooked old man
you never thought he'd become.
Feel your heels sink into the earth
with every sorry step you take.
Weave your way through the graves
of strangers who will keep your mother
company forever: the Greenblatts,
the Goldbergs, the Shapiros, the Steins.
Stop at a small mountain of dirt
next to a hole that holds the plain pine box
that holds what's left of your mother.
Listen to the rabbi mumble
prayers you've heard a hundred times
but this time offer no comfort.
Smell the sweet honeysuckle breeze
that is making your stomach buckle.
Feel the sun bake your little black dress.
Wait for the rabbi to close
his little black book.
Bring your father close to the earth
that is waiting to blanket your mother.
Watch him shove the shovel
into the mound upside down
showing the world how distasteful
this last task is.
See him dump clumps of soil

onto your mother's casket.
Hear the dull thuds
of your heart hammering your chest.
Watch how your father plants the shovel
into the silent pile of dirt
and then walks off
slumped over like a man
who finally admits defeat.
Step up to the mound.
Grasp the shovel firmly.
Lift it up and feel the warm wood
between your two damp hands.
Jab the shovel into the soil.
Toss the hard brown lumps
into that dark gaping hole.
Hear the dirt rain down upon your mother.
Surrender
the shovel to your brother.
Drag yourself away.
Do not look back.

I CARRY MY MOTHER

I carry my mother wherever I go
Her belly, her thighs, her plentiful hips
Her milky white skin she called this side of snow
The crease of her brow and the plump of her lips

Her belly, her thighs, her plentiful hips
The curl of her hair and her sharp widow's peak
The crease of her brow and the plump of her lips
The hook of her nose and the curve of her cheek

The curl of her hair and her sharp widow's peak
The dark beauty mark to the left of her chin
The hook of her nose and the curve of her cheek
Her delicate wrist so impossibly thin

The dark beauty mark to the left of her chin
Her deep set brown eyes that at times appeared black
Her delicate wrist so impossibly thin
I stare at the mirror, my mother stares back

Her deep set brown eyes that at times appeared black
Her milky white skin she called this side of snow
I stare at the mirror, my mother stares back
I carry my mother wherever I go

KRISTEN STONE

XXXX

EXCERPTS FROM
FAMILY HISTORY, OR, HOW TO WRITE A GHOST
(WORK IN PROGRESS)

#1, Virginia before

Once the mother went to college. At the University of California in Berkeley. She was upright in her posture, manners, and good name. She dressed in the style of the day, lived with her parents who were harsh but fair, a prominent local family who made their money in oil. Her IQ had consistently tested over 140 on the longevity study she and her sister participated in once every 2 years from the time they were born. Asked to hug the wire monkey or the soft monkey that made a bad sound she performed impressively. They were asked to crawl over a glass plate, that had a steep drop off, to their mothers. Most of the babies just sat there and cried, presumably because they thought they would fall if they went towards the mothers, who looked like an advertisement for soap or something pleasing, all the smart mothers of Berkeley in their bright colored skirts, cooing at their angry babies on the glass plate. Or maybe they cried because crawling hurt, or the light hurt, or because their mothers were cold and unfeeling. We can't really know because babies can't talk. For all these reasons Virginia knew she was intelligent. It was expected she would attend college, teach primary school for a year or two and then marry the nice young man who comes over on Sunday afternoons.

#2, *Virginia after*

She is lying in bed listening to her husband leave for work. Her eyes won't focus, or will only focus on the handfuls of sheets clutched in front of her face. She could sit up, put on the glasses she wears to keep her headaches at bay—they are sitting on the night table, right within reach, but she doesn't. She hears him pour the second cup of coffee and shut the door, she hears the engine charge into time and back down the driveway. The bedroom is dim but the light coming in slits through the wavering mini blinds is already hot and bright, high in the sky, it feels like the sun defies the rest of the cosmos in this hot place near the wrong ocean. She's hot under there, tangled in the sheets and her nightgown. She's glad her husband is gone but this means a long hot day of the children, one making trouble, the other creepy and still, like a doll. The grocery list on the counter weighs a thousand pounds. Putting the children in the car, driving to the shopping center, the hot seats of the car leaving sweaty red welts on the backs of their thighs, the air conditioning in the supermarket, selecting item after item all the shames and textures, endless experiences bright and mundane, making the children put on clothes and eat food and turn the television down, a thousand things that would have to happen, and happen, and happen. She hates this hot bright place with grass in stiff squares, where you are only ever inside or outside and both are too bright and the wrong temperature. She came from a place where the colors are proper, and the temperatures are in balance, like a hand-tinted photograph, the ocean is cold and frightening and full of rocks and ugly brown sea lions, the houses were on hills and many things were old, properly old—the University of California, her parents' house and their money. Now she lives in a flat bright place with a gray bathwater ocean and sand like a litter box or construction site, an enormous sky just raining down light all day, she can't hide and when she's away from the children she just worries: sends them out to play and imagines them hurt or snatched or smashed. She's still in the dark— the last remaining bit of dark for the entire day—and already her head throbs.

Why did she marry a scientist who married the rockets they shoot off next to the sea? Her nightgown is damp and she has the sense that she's rotting from the inside. When she first married how worried she was, all the private things about the body you can't hide in a house, in a marriage, a shared bed. Her armpits, also damp, smell like paint chips or barbecue, and her teeth are filmy. How long would she have to stay until they couldn't recognize her, before child services came and took them away, before her husband moved to the space center, pulverized himself and sent the dust up to space.

She's met some of the astronauts' wives, and is jealous of them, the fear they get to nurture, so brave and their husbands away in a tiny rocket orbiting the earth and then falling, detached at the right instance, falling miles through the sky and dropping into the ocean to be scooped up by ship or whale. Why not hers, so noble and far away, why did he have to come back each evening?

She's bleeding through her nightgown and onto the sheet. She doesn't care.

She feels how her daughter recoils from her, how their exchanges of affection are brief and rote. Her son she doesn't try. He spins wildly off to climb things, break things, set twigs and bits of paper on fire.

Why is she like this?

#3, the girl who later went away

Sandy hated the light but she loved the heat, this made her worry that she was a ghost or a kind of demon. She would lie under the bed, the backs of her knees sweating against the scratchy carpet, its new chemical smell rising and burning her nose, hot wet insides. Dry scratchy cave for a hot moist body under the bed. She would pick her scabs under there, working a ragged thumbnail under the hard dry edge to the point of resistance in the middle where the skin wasn't ready yet, then yank. She would lick the new skin underneath. She would suck the skin until it was wet and hotter and redder than before.

When her mother asked what she was doing under there, she would say, reading.

This was not a lie. She would take her mother's paperback novels out of the bathroom, where they stood in a stack next to the toilet. Books for shitting. She imagined the cheap paper soaked up the smells of shit and bleach and hairspray. She tried not to think of her mother with her giant fake silk underwear around her ankles reading about throbbing and slick and overcome and grunting and moaning. It felt like the most private thing in the world, to be in the cave under the bed, pricking with sweat, reading the books, which were similar enough that they lulled her into a slight fever. It seemed like all that ever existed was Sandy, under the bed with these predictable books.

Outside the sun was bright and hot, her mother took her brother to the pool and he came back panting and green-damp, hair plastered to his head.

#4, the girl who went away, years later

Many years later a detective contacts her. She's at work maybe waitressing or bartending or working at a nursing home or hospital, exhausting work for tired women in uniforms. Whichever job it is involves heavy lifting, getting damp, being polite. (I can't see far enough into the future, I am gifted, but all gifts have limits.) The detective asks if her name is A********* S****, if she was adopted in Washington State as an infant in 1957, if she is estranged from her family of origin. All these things she can say yes to, but she gives herself away as someone afraid by asking who wants to know. Your younger brother has hired me to find you.

(My mother says that she was 'fragile,' that he was 'cruel.' She'd had a heart attack and a stroke. She didn't understand why he'd contact her, and didn't remember anything that he wanted to know, so he threw her away quickly. She was going to get him a nice room at the Holiday Inn in Iowa or Nebraska or South Dakota, she lives out west, but my mother was vague about that too).

#5, *the night before the funeral*

I pull a tarot card for her. I pull the empress reversed. I look her up on the internet: troubled mothering and disarray. Wrong time, failed domesticity, messy house.

My father actually said this afternoon that she "passed over." I cringed. He sounded so New Age, at lunch over apple fritters and fried egg sandwiches, showing off his goodness for my great aunt, his nice family, his suburban town's excellent selection of strip mall restaurants. My father is pious but the look passes over his face. I used to think of that look, a cloud passing over, as a gray angel.

The tarot is exhausting, to choose a meaning from the tiny white book. In the morning I will not remember these feelings right.

Empress reversed: the longest running cocktail party in history, my father eating cheese and crackers for dinner in a cloud of what they now call secondhand smoke.

TAKING JASMINE TO ANASTASIA ISLAND STATE PARK FOR HER 27TH BIRTHDAY

i wait outside the bathroom for you at the state park.
i hang my long frame over the railing. why do we call a body a frame. i use the word without thinking. Real Women Have Curves. i have angles and ankles, nervous hands. i am outside woman and i am okay with that. there is a tension to being a dyke. not a binary tension but something else. one person has to be something else. to wait outside with the picnic. the sky is so big here near the beach, the wind pulls my dirty hair and balloons my windbreaker with the broken zipper, it makes me edgy. the blue and white. i squint and lean my foot on something and stretch absentmindedly. a weak boyfriend.

once somebody called me genderqueer
i didn't know what they meant. i am a bad butch because i don't take up space. i am a bad radical because i like for people to have manners. (i am a social worker, which precludes a total rejection of institutions, so i cannot be That Cool.) the tension of being a dyke is something else, not like i imagine heterosexuality. i am the boyfriend because of my short hair and pegged pants and i drive the car when we go places, but i am also the wife, i want the baby and keep the house and lie still so you can fuck me. i mean, fuck me please, with your thick hips and soft white tits and long golden hair. i comb the knots out of it, like a governess or mother. sometimes when you fuck me you wear a harness that looks like stretchy boys' underwear, with a gaping plastic mouth to hold the cock.

once my therapist called me a lesbian.
and i looked at her blankly. i don't think i like that word, i told her. i am not a lesbian; i don't have gay pride; i identify with shame. not gay shame but being a prude. the only person who knows what i mean by this hates me now. that's an ugly loneliness.

you come out of the bathroom and i go in.

there should be a separation between couples and maybe it has to do with the bathroom, maybe it has to do with tasks, doors, fluids. bodies at their least cute. the bathroom is damp and loud because there's a hand dryer. i hate hand dryers and wipe the water off on my pants.

point
i feel outside woman in a metaphysical, melancholy way. i'm not sure if it's about femininity or the phallus or what. maybe it's linguistic or psychoanalytic and all women feel this way. i don't think it's interesting or relevant or has anything much to do with patriarchy or oppression. some people will read this and contest my feeling outside woman altogether because so many people are further outside woman but all i can say is this essay is not about that.

this essay is about taking jasmine to the state park on her 27th birthday which means it's about the cultural creation of picnics. i like picnics and my father hates them because they are a lot of work. my father is a True Capitalist. i like that it is non-rational to pack up your food and dishes, take them somewhere, eat at a hard picnic table in the wind or sun, and then take it all back home. i have faith in things that are clumsy and must defend themselves. i have faith in things that are non-rational.

counterpoint
i say all this then i think the picnic, like the pastoral, relies on industrialization while setting itself in opposition to it. you have to make people stay inside all the time for a picnic to make sense, really. so a picnic relies on capitalism even as it seems outside it. we talk around these things lazily, as we squint in the sun and follow the boardwalk over the dunes. sounding uselessly smart is a thing we do without really noticing, like scratching at dandruff or getting up in the night to pee.

we sit on the cold bright sand for awhile and kiss.

in florida you're not supposed to go in the dunes because of erosion; in michigan you can. this has caused some tension in our relationship, your trying to climb these dunes, here. here, the beach is falling into itself like a toothless mouth. we have hurricanes and the high-rises could fall into the sea. you might step in a hidden clutch of soft turtle eggs. in michigan the dunes are soft white mountains, and in winter the lake-waves freeze into giant boulders on shore.

i need to stop writing about michigan or this essay will never end.
we walk back up the beach, and over the boardwalk, we put the rest of the picnic into my car, we climb a lighthouse, we drive home.

Franciszka Voeltz

Trouble Works in This Body

POETXT 12

we slowdance this
machine into
armache and atrophy
while streaming
threads of fever and
fuck. use this
quarter inch of
lifeforce under a
whole thankyou sky.

SIX KILOMETERS

rainsounds
on neighbor's specklegray roof

there are some places
where women walk an hour or two
to fill five-gallon jerrycans
with clean water

there are some places positioned
between home and clean water
that qualify as hostile territory

there are some hostile territories that qualify
a women's body as fair game
with or without the weight of water
drawing out the muscles in her forearms

POETXT 11

economic downturn
the dancemove undo.
trouble works in this
body, your house.
straddling early, this
modernism needs
some serious ass
tonight. understudy
a glove

CONSIDER THE SOUP CAN

consider the wooden plunger handle
in a four-storey house in the bronx on osborne place
october third, 2010
consider the shaving cream can
the baseball bat

when given the choice
between that and a metal pipe
-if you could pull language up
from the well of your chest-
which would you choose?
and would you wonder
how many meanings exist
within that word as it falls
from your mouth

bat = new york yankees
    = flying mammals
bat =
bat = eyelashes flickering
    = to strike
bat = please
    = don't kill me
bat =
    =
    =

consider, like the shaving cream can,
the soup can
on october third 2002
in newark, california
consider the jury considering
the "trans panic" defense

(when i found out her
body was different from
what i expected i panicked
and killed her with a soup can
a frying pan
a shovel)

consider a 179-part chorus of sharp
air intake from lungs never
expected to rise again

like the sound of a tsunami
saltwater sucked out to sea

POETXT 4

i think i can bind you
breathing in. summer
stones smoothed. the
treehouse. the skin.
undone by skyscrape
over other under.
stillness waiting.
in miniature

WHEN YOU DREAM OF A HOUSE, THE HOUSE REPRESENTS YOUR BODY

"there used to be no house, hardly a room, in which someone had not died . . . today, people live in rooms that have never been touched by death." - walter benjamin

A

alphabet—
i'm trying to build a bridge
to (name of the place you are)
by laying letters out next to each other
so i can walk across and see
your face

B

bones—
to know that we have built museums of joy
in our marrow

C

chemotherapy—
and all of this is to say
how is it possible
to write about anything else
than your mother's bones

G

gravity—
body thrown in a dumpster
dumped on a sidewalk

charred torso found in a ditch
we can light candles
and read each name aloud

part litany
part incantation

N

new age music—
it took my mom three hours to die
she tells me
and they asked me to d.j.
so i looked through her collection

noon—
you will catch the sound of bells
carried on air around you

P

passage (and other birds)—
1. seagull with wounded leg
at the edge of campsite thirty
like a chicken sits in its roost
you toss out ricecake crumbs

2. street-found
ant-eaten
fly-covered
baby bird shimmering

3. 400 canada geese rounded up in prospect park, brooklyn
euthanized, double bagged and dumped
in a landfill in the name of air safety

T

time—
1. finger travels roughcut edges counting
67 rings from the center out
suspended over snowmelt river

2. nikolai told me how the life spans of those who
work graveyard are 1/3 shorter
than those who don't

3. nine years ago today full moon
when you fastened the rope
and slipped your bare feet
from the branch
in the palo alto hills
which is another way of saying
i have not forgotten / will never forget
your handwriting
our boot dance
rolling back dried vines
to dig up duck-shaped sweet potatoes
under september sun
pressing apples into cold sweet juice
in the outdoor kitchen at your side

W

water—
headed north on the 205 then east on the 14
towards clear cold washougal river
we discover four out of our five fathers
are vietnam vets
one worked in construction
erecting barracks, rebuilding bombed out villages
photos of black-haired kids

eating white rice from wide bowls
a metal film canister filled with vietnamese coins
a story of how the sun burned his body so bad he blistered
and a story of a river bridge for hotweather diving
the surprise of a body
floating by

i have asked
vietnamese or american
but i have never asked
clothed or flesh
face down or up
i have never asked
who was there
to collect ID tags
fingerprints
teeth

POETXT 16

glimmer the weather
for me. send scandal to
drift overnight. air it
out. allow the
guttwist to sleep.
honor fracture this
body offer warm up
to boxing ring dream.

NOTES:

poetxts:
each poetxt was written using the predictive text function on a
sanyo katana flip phone that allows only 160 characters per each
text.

six kilometers is the average distance women in parts of africa
and asia walk to collect clean water. these women face the
frequent risk of sexual assault and rape on their journies.

consider the soup can:
on october 3, 2010, three men, based on the grounds that they
were suspected to be gay, were assaulted in an abandoned
apartment building in the bronx. one of the survivors was given
the choice to be beaten with a bat or a lead pipe.

on october 3, 2002, gwen araujo was strangled with rope and
beaten to death with a soup can, a shovel, and a frying pan by
four men she knew after they discovered she was transgendered.
The men were convicted of second-degree murder but were not
charged with hate crime enhancements after claiming "trans
panic" in defense.

179 is the reported number of trans people killed worldwide in
2010 due to anti-transgender hatred or prejudice.

CINDY BAKER

COVER ARTIST

SELF-PORTRAITS OF MY HAND LOUNGING NAKED IN BED

I've been working on a series of photographs exploring fat women and sexuality (the working title is "Self-portraits of my hand lounging naked in bed.") Through it, I am trying to evoke the dual sensations of attraction and repulsion inherent in our society's relationship to fat women, creating ridiculous bodyscapes using only my hand. These farcical sexscapes, intended to be mistaken for other, larger bodyparts, will remain, to the average viewer, alien even after they come to understand what the subject of the photographs is because our collective denial of the fat woman's body includes all of her parts, including her hands.

Taken with a now-obsolete first-generation Sony Mavica digital camera with a macro lens capable of shooting screen-quality images only, the obvious pixellation foregrounds the digital medium and uses it as a barrier to the subject.

The natural lighting and pictures taken at various times during the day are meant to suggest a comfortable, placid environment, and a day filled with self-indulgent lounging. The subject of a partner or a second body is never broached, except when the viewer imagines one amidst the creases and rolls. This atmosphere set up through the series subtly confirms our learned suppositions of fat women as self-indulgent, and resists confrontationalism by refusing to suggest the viewer's role in this taboo sexcapade, thus allowing us to let our guard down enough to explore the attraction/repulsion element of the physicality of the body, which we normally are forbidden from engaging.

CONTRIBUTORS

Interdisciplinary and performance artist **CINDY BAKER [COVER ARTIST]** is passionate about gender culture, queer theory, fat activism, and art theory. Baker considers context her primary medium, working with whatever materials are needed to allow her to concentrate on the theoretical, conceptual, and ephemeral aspects of her work. Fiercely committed to her diverse communities, Baker has a 2-decade long background of working, volunteering, and sitting on the board for several artist-run centres and non-profits in Western Canada. While enjoying lecturing and publishing in academic contexts, Baker has also done work as diverse as presenting workshops at Interpride in San Francisco, organizing screenings for a furry convention in San Jose and modeling for life drawing classes with transgender porn star Buck Angel. Her volunteer work in the art and queer communities of which she has been a member has directly influenced Baker's work, and her ability to move fluently among and between the arts, humanities, and social science disciplines that make up her field of research. Based out of Lethbridge, Alberta, where she is pursuing an MFA at the University of Lethbridge, Baker has exhibited and performed across Canada and internationally.

JUDITH BARRINGTON recently won the Gregory O'Donoghue Poetry Prize and gave a reading in Cork (Ireland). She has published three poetry collections, most recently *Horses and the Human Soul* and two chapbooks: *Postcard from the Bottom of the Sea* and *Lost Lands* (winner of the Robin Becker Chapbook Award for LGBT poets). Her memoir, *Lifesaving*, won the Lambda Literary Award and was a finalist for the PEN/Martha Albrand Award. She also won the ACLU of Oregon's Freedom of Expression Award. She has taught for the University of Alaska's MFA Program and at workshops across the US, Britain, and Spain. Born and raised in England, she moved to Oregon in 1976 where she lives with her partner of 34 years.

ELA BARTON is a queer poet and artist living in Seattle, Washington. She is the 2007 Bainbridge Island Annual Poetry Slam Champion, a four-time finalist of the Seattle Poetry Slam Grand Slam and the first woman to win Jack McCarthy's Evergreen Invitational (2011). Barton has taught Creative Writing and Performance Poetry at Bent: A Queer Writing Institute. She is the current Co-Slammaster and Founder of Rain City Poetry Slam. Barton was described in Seattle Gay News by Shaun Knittel as "unapologetic, smart, and sharp-tongued—nothing seemed immune to her poignant observations." Author, Poet, and Activist Tara Hardy said, "Ela Barton is the queer echo to the first whisper of revolution. Backlash to cynicism, she'll have you believing in yourself again."

Born in Trinidad and raised in New York City, **CHERYL BOYCE-TAYLOR** is the curator of The Calypso Muse Reading Series. The author of three poetry collections, *Raw Air, Night When Moon Follows*, and *Convincing the Body*. Cheryl's poems are installed in Diane Samuel's Lines of Sight, a permanent exhibit at Brown University in Rhode Island. Her poems are published in numerous anthologies including: *The World In Us: Lesbian and Gay Poetry of the Next Wave, A Woman Like That, ALOUD: Voices from the Nuyorican Poets Cafe, The Mom Egg, To Be Left With the Body, Caribbean Erotica*, and upcoming in Red Beard Press. A graduate of Stonecoast MFA Poetry Program, Cheryl's poetry has been commissioned by the National Endowment for the Arts for Ronald K. Brown/Evidence Dance Company and for Jacobs Pillow and The Joyce Theater for Dance.

ELIZABETH BRADFIELD is the author of two poetry collections: *Approaching Ice* and *Interpretive Work*. Her poems have appeared in *The Atlantic, Orion, The Believer, Poetry,* and she has been awarded the Audre Lorde Prize and a Stegner Fellowship, among other honors. Founder and editor-in-chief of Broadsided Press, she lives on Cape Cod and works as a naturalist and teacher. She is the current Poet-in-Residence at Brandeis University.

CHING-IN CHEN is author of *The Heart's Traffic* (Arktoi Books/Red Hen Press) and co-editor of *The Revolution Starts at Home: Confronting Intimate Violence Within Activist Communities* (South End Press). They are a Kundiman, Lambda, and Norman Mailer Poetry Fellow and a member of the Voices of Our Nations Arts Foundation and Macondo writing communities. A community organizer, they have worked in the Asian American communities of San Francisco, Oakland, Riverside, and Boston. In Milwaukee, they are *cream city review*'s editor-in-chief. www.chinginchen.com

MEG DAY, recently selected for *Best New Poets of 2013*, is a 2013 recipient of an NEA Fellowship in Poetry and the author of *Last Psalm at Sea Level,* winner of the Barrow Street Press Poetry Prize (forthcoming 2014), *When All You Have Is a Hammer* (winner of the 2012 Gertrude Press Chapbook Contest), and *We Can't Read This* (winner of the 2013 Gazing Grain Chapbook Contest). A 2012 AWP Intro Journals Award Winner, she has also received awards and fellowships from the Lambda Literary Foundation, Hedgebrook, Squaw Valley Writers, and the International Queer Arts Festival. Meg is currently a PhD fellow in Poetry & Disability Poetics at the University of Utah. www.megday.com.

LAURA HERSHEY was a Colorado poet, writer, and a crip, feminist, queer activist. Her chapbook *Spark Before Dark* was published in 2011. She obtained her MFA at Antioch University and was a Lambda Literary Fellow. Her poems have appeared in *Calyx, Shakespeare's Monkey Review, Trillium Literary Journal, make/shift,* and *www.wordgathering.com* as well as the anthologies *Fire in the Soul: 100 Poems for Human Rights* and *Beauty as a Verb*. She wrote essays for *Ms., off our backs, Waccamaw Journal, National Parks, U.S. News & World Report,* and many other publications. Hershey died in late 2010. More of her work can be seen at www.laurahershey.com.

JP HOWARD aka Juliet P. Howard is a poet, Cave Canem graduate fellow, member of The Hot Poets Collective, and native New Yorker. She co-founded Women Writers in Bloom Poetry Salon and Blog (WWBPS), a forum offering women writers at all levels a venue to come together in a positive and supportive space. WWBPS hosts monthly literary salons in New York and the blog accepts submissions of poetry. JP was a Lambda Literary Foundation 2012 and 2011 Emerging LGBT Voices Fellow, as well as a Cave Canem

2011 Fellow in Residence at the Virginia Center for the Creative Arts. She was a 2009-2010 finalist in the poetry category by the Lesbian Writer's Fund of Astraea Lesbian Foundation for Justice. She was also the recipient of a Soul Mountain Retreat writing residency in 2010. Her poems have been published or are forthcoming in: *The Best American Poetry Blog, MiPOesias iPad Companion, African Voices Magazine, Kweli Journal, The Mom Egg* 2013 & 2012, *Talking Writing, Muzzle Magazine, Muzzle's* 2011 "Best of the First Year" print issue, *Connotation Press, Brown Girl Love*, an online writing project for women of color, *TORCH, Queer Convention: A Chapbook of Fierce, Cave Canem Anthology XII: Poems 2008-2009, Cave Canem XI 2007 Anthology, Promethean Literary Journal, The Portable Lower East Side (Queer City)*, and *Poetry in Performance*. She was awarded an MFA in Creative Writing from the City College of New York in 2009, holds a BA from Barnard College as well as a JD from Brooklyn Law School. http://womenwritersinbloompoetrysalon. blogspot.com

JOY LADIN is the author of six books of poetry: recently published *The Definition of Joy*, Lambda Literary Award finalist *Transmigration*, Forward Fives award winner *Coming to Life, Alternatives to History* and *The Book of Anna* (all from Sheep Meadow Press), and *Psalms* (Wipf & Stock). Her memoir, *Through the Door of Life: A Jewish Journey Between Genders*, was a 2012 National Jewish Book Award finalist. Her work has appeared or is forthcoming in many periodicals, including *American Poetry Review, Prairie Schooner, Southern Review, Parnassus: Poetry in Review, Southwest Review, Michigan Quarterly Review*, and *North American Review*. She holds the David and Ruth Gottesman Chair in English at Stern College of Yeshiva University.

M. MACK is a genderqueer poet and editor in or around Washington, D.C. Ze holds an MFA from George Mason University and is former managing editor of *So to Speak: a feminist journal of language and art*. Mack's work has appeared recently in *APARTMENT Poetry Quarterly, Gargoyle*, and *Wicked Alice* and is forthcoming in the anthology *The Queer South* (Sibling Rivalry Press, 2014). Ze is founding co-editor of Gazing Grain Press, an explicitly inclusive feminist chapbook press.

LESLÉA NEWMAN is the author of 63 books for readers of all ages including the poetry collections, *Nobody's Mother, Still Life with Buddy*, and *Signs of*

Love. Other titles include the short story collection, *A Letter to Harvey Milk,* the novel, *The Reluctant Daughter,* and the children's book, *Heather Has Two Mommies.* Her newest book, *October Mourning: A Song for Matthew Shepard* is a novel-in-verse that explores the impact of Matthew Shepard's murder in a cycle of 68 poems. Lesléa's literary awards include poetry fellowships from the National Endowment for the Arts and the Massachusetts Artist Fellowship Foundation. A past poet laureate of Northampton, Massachusetts, she teaches at Spalding University's brief-residency MFA in Writing Program. Currently she is working on a poetry collection entitled *I Carry My Mother.*

KRISTEN STONE is the author of *Domestication Handbook* (Rogue Factorial, 2012) and the editor of Unthinkable Creatures Chapbook Press. Her poetry and essays have appeared in *Finery, 30xlace, Women's Studies Quarterly, 3:AM,* and elsewhere. Kristen lives in Gainesville, Florida, where she is a social worker, teacher, and freelance editor. Read her blog at future-imaginary.tumblr.com.

The question, is it possible that poems can do things? For instance, can they undo the racist capitalist heteropatriachy we live under? As a community writing workshop facilitator, **FRANCISZKA VOELTZ** has witnessed poems affecting subtler change. As a poet who believes in writing as social practice, Voeltz is invested in writing that disrupts and agitates and language that connects and heals. Franciszka has been reading and writing about water and curates a collective poem to the entire planet at dearbelovedsproject. wordpress.com. She maintains a daily writing practice (the detail collector) on the world wide web and her poems have appeared in various publications including A*nalecta Literary Journal, Ocho,* and *Flaneur Foundry.* She is the recipient of several poetry fellowhips including those granted by the Helene Wurlitzer Foundation and Art Farm. Voeltz received an MFA in Writing from the University of California, San Diego.

VALERIE WETLAUFER [Editor of *Adrienne*] is a poet, doula, editor, and teacher. Her first full-length poetry collection *Mysterious Acts by My People* will be published by Sibling Rivalry Press in March 2014. She lives in Iowa.

CPSIA information can be obtained at www.ICGtesting.com
Printed in the USA
LVOW13s2113291213

367346LV00002B/4/P